I Call
You
Friend

I Call You Friend

By Perry Tanksley

Allgood Books

BOX 1329

JACKSON, MISSISSIPPI 39205

Manufactured by THE PARTHENON PRESS
201 8th Ave. South, Nashville, Tenn., U.S.A.

I call you friend for that portrays my feeling,
And it, upon reflection, is a word appealing.
Friend, you've shared my joys and in my troubles, helped.
You've laughed when I rejoiced and suffered when I wept.
I call you friend for this depicts so true
What I would like to be if I could be like you.*

I Call You Friend

If we knew tonight we had our last chance for decades
To see the stars displayed, I think we'd gaze and gaze.
If we knew sight was failing and soon we would be blind,
We'd gaze for days at beauty and hold it in our minds.
If we knew today would be our last day of good health,
We'd spend it visiting friends, sharing affection we'd felt.

* This poem and all poems and prose in this volume were written by Perry Tanksley.

CAN ONE VIEW CREATION

How can one look at stars,
Or tread a tree-fringed sod,
Or hear birds sing at dawn
And say there is no God?
How can one scan the sea,
Or ride an ocean breaker,
Or view a far-off mountain
And swear there is no Maker?
How can one view creation
And not feel like a traitor
While arrogantly insisting
There is no Creator?

LIFE IS LIKE THIS

He lived on a mountain
Where very few men
Ever ventured or camped
Because the air was thin.
But he loved the view
From the mountain side
Of the gold sunset
And the early sunrise.
Sometimes for the valley
He'd leave the tall hills
And share with the folk
What a mountain-dweller feels.
They laughed at his story
And mocked his appearance.
All valley-dwellers doubt
What mountain men experience.

WHEN COUNTING FOR SOMETHING

A boy longing to count for something
Passed by a leaking dike
And sensed his life-time chance had come
To count and be useful-like.
He saw and quickly took his chance
To save the Netherlands
By plugging a very tiny leak
Using one finger on a hand.
Through the frozen night he stood fast
Crying aloud for help
And willing if it were necessary
To sacrifice himself
Dutchmen claim he saved their country.
And when nursed back to life
He said, "When counting for something,
Boys don't mind sacrifice."

A NAME KNOWN TO GOD

I searched the world to find earth's most heroic name;
I scanned thick history books; I probed vast halls of fame.
I pondered martyrs buried beneath church spires and steeples;
I wept by shrines of freedom where patriots died for people.
I searched until I found a fact revealed to few:
The true and great heroes, historians never knew
Unpraised, most heroes lived and oft laid down their lives
With none to note their deeds of bravery facing strife.
None knew the wounds they bore, for brave men don't complain;
No markers mark their graves and no one knows their names.
Yet I think God takes note of those who without praise,
Stood at their post of duty and struggled through life's days.
I searched and found the bravest, at least most all of them,
Possessed names known to God and only known to Him.

BUT HE IS WITH US NOW

If Christ came in the flesh to visit us again
He'd bring no brand new message; He'd say, "Be born again."
If Christ were to return our modern world to tread,
He'd give no fresh command; He'd say what He once said.
If Christ by chance came now to face our common lot,
He'd come with no new teaching; He'd say, "Trust Me, fear not."
But is He not with us as sure as long ago?
And does He not still speak through scriptures that we know?
We hear today each time we read the sacred page
The self-same words of Jesus as in that ancient age.

FOR LOVE OF BEAUTY

From piles of stone and lumber, two brothers took some boards
And built on lots adjoining the best they could afford.
One brother built with skill and a lot of planning
From the lumber provided, an elegant mansion.
The other built a hovel out of identical material
Because he lacked a plan and had no building skill.
In life we're character-building and oft from gifts the same,
One builds for love of beauty, another builds to shame.

SIXTY YEARS OF GRACE

An artist made a portrait of one forlorn of youth,
Yet wrinkles in her face were lines of love and truth.
As she left, a young girl asked, "What reason or what rhyme
Should make one so wrinkled use up an artist's time?"
The artist scanned the critic but saw unkindness there
Though she was young and tender and very, very fair.
He smiled, "We artists see a beauty hid to eye,
Her face revealed God's love, a kindness I admire.
Surely the Master-artist through sixty years of grace,
Has made a masterpiece of that dear lady's face."

STARVING FOR ROSES

Lord, we appreciate
The daily bread you give,
But now we know it takes
Much more than bread to live.
For life is difficult
With duty it imposes,
And though we crave the bread,
We're starving for some roses.
In other words, dear Lord,
Let love enhance each duty—
And life blend with romance;
And with our bread give beauty.

THE REAL ATHEISM

To affirm your faith and quote the creed,
And then hate an enemy, is atheism, indeed.
To attend church often and then to turn
To doubt and worry, is atheism confirmed.
To profess Christ's name and go on cheating
Is not Christianity, but atheism succeeding.

BROKEN LIMBS

Old apple trees with broken limbs
Possess a certain beauty,
For limbs break down from bearing fruit
Beyond the call of duty.
So beauty of that sort abides
With one of my good neighbors;
Like weighted limbs I watched him break,
Bowed down with fruitful labors.
Yet some who pass, not knowing why
Fruit limbs crash to the ground,
May see no beauty in my friend
Or in trees broken down.

MY UNREACHED IDEAL

To feel and heal men's hurts
Is my ideal for living.
To walk with common people
Is my supreme ambition;
To have the common touch,
To love their unloved souls,
To lift one fallen person
Is my high, shining goal.
To practice what I preach
And feel what all men feel
Is my supreme ambition
And my unreached ideal.

UNCOUNTED BLESSINGS

I've known the curse of doubts and borne my share of fears,
And I've endured despair and shed my share of tears.
But looking back I've learned at least one cherished lesson:
My woes are small compared to all my myraid blessings.
Still I ungrateful fret while blessings high have mounted
Because possessed with fears, my blessings go uncounted.

I'LL BYPASS DEATH

When I die let no one cry.
You know I can't stand crying.
And let none weep because I sleep
Or say I dreaded dying.
Should any grieve because I leave,
Please know I enjoyed living,
And let friends know I gladly go
Forgiven and forgiving.
Then let none groan when I pass on
To be with friends I cherish;
With my last breath I'll bypass death
Nevermore to perish

THE QUESTION

A path on which men walked each day
Said to a rose crushed by the way,
"You smell so sweet! How can it be?"
The rose replied, "Men walk on me."
"They walk on me," the sad path wept,
"But it makes me harder each step."
I pondered this until I asked,
"Am I the rose or like the path?"

⚜

MY UNBROKEN HEART

Regardless of cost I sought to avoid
The tragic hurt of being annoyed
With a broken heart from loving someone
To discover too late, my love unreturned.
Alas, I discovered while living alone,
My heart unbroken had turned to stone.

⚜

HELPING PEOPLE IN THE WRONG WAY

Because I had no time
To teach him how to fish,
I fed the beggar, trout
And blue-gill on a dish.
Too tired to share my faith
With him who had a crutch
I shared, instead, some coins
And he thanked me very much.
With ease I urged my child,
"Depend on me alone,"
'Til sheltered years left him
Without a faith his own.

UNTIL WE SEE HIS CROSS

He was not born in palace halls
But in a crude-built manger.
He did not come in kingly garb
But as a baby stranger.
He did not live in public view
But in a wayside place;
The Lord of Life disguished Himself
To join the human race.
How strange they did not know their King
Until His life was lost;
How strange we, too, know not the Lord
Until we see His cross.

THE OVERFLOW

Once God so filled me I felt I could not stand such abundance,
So I prayed, "Dear God, withhold Thy hand."
A thousand times I've wished I could recall that hour
And feel again the Presence, and sense the Spirit's power.
I'd pray, "Enlarge me, Lord, and let Thy blessings pour,"
But most of all I'd pray, "Dear God, let me run o'er."

KILLING CHILDHOOD DREAMS

May I not be accused
Of planned or unplanned scheming
To crush my children's dreams
When they're caught up with dreaming.
For there's no viler deed
Parents ever do
Than killing childhood dreams,
Saying they can't come true.
Lord, let me with my children,
Searching for the truth,
Encourage dreaming dreams
As I dreamed in my youth.

THE OLD HEARTHSTONE

From childhood's vanished years
On memory's golden wings
There floats to my mind's eye
Some cherished childhood scenes.
The scene I love the best
While musing all alone
Is of my family dear
Circling the old hearthstone.
Back then when day was done,
Around that old fireplace
We'd sit and talk, while flames
Cast shadows on our face.
Fireplaces meant so much;
Our country needs them now
With families joining hands
Around hearthstones of prayer.

HE'S LEFT FOOTPRINTS

God made this universe
And none of us can grasp
How stars were sprayed through space.
Oh, what a wondrous task!
He scooped the valleys out
And stacked the mountains up,
And tacked His carpet green
With fragrant buttercups.
And He's left footprints here
On sky and sea and sod,
And only men born blind
Dare say there is no God.

A DOUBLE DOSE OF COURAGE

It startled me at first!
Yet by a mountain stream
I saw a blind man painting
A golden sunset scene.
At first I stood amazed,
Yet one with fingers gone
Was strumming his guitar
And humming low a song.
It seemed incredible!
Yet one who lost her child
Stood up in praise of God
And through her tears she smiled.
"Impossible," I said.
Yet sipping sorrow's cup
I saw a widow go
To cheer her neighbors up.
I doubted it at first,
Yet going to his store
My wheel-chair neighbor smiled
Each day he passed my door.
How grand that God pours out
On those crushed down with sadness
A double dose of courage,
An extra cup of gladness.

IT CAN'T BE DONE

I most admire him who can cry
"It can't be done but I will try."
Who shouts as he his goal pursues,
"What can't be done is what I'll do!"
Who sings this song once he's begun,
"I do the things which can't be done!"
And then exclaims with joy unhid,
"What can't be done is what I did,"

MEN WANTED

Of squeamish-minded men
I want to have no part,
And men with priggish views
So niggardly at heart.
For pygmy-minded men
Embracing midget goals
Squelch cherished faith from me
Just as they blight all souls.
Of stingy-minded men
My weary heart is tiring;
God, give us braver men,
Great-hearted and inspiring.

TO BY-PASS DISCOURAGEMENT

Dear Lord, exempt me not from life and death and judgment.
I can take all of it but I can't take discouragement.
I do not seek smooth paths, my skies need not be fair,
But in the struggle, Lord, exempt me from despair.
Grant me such gladness, Lord, and peace amidst the strife
That I'll by-pass discouragement that saps the strength from life.

WHERE I FOUND GOD

With scorn I built a wall
Excluding undersirables,
And I, shut-in with God,
Re-read all of my Bibles.
I had misgivings though
And so, one day in doubt
I climbed my wall to see
Vile things I had shut out.
'Twas there amidst outcasts
I saw the Lord of All—
The God I thought I had
Confined behind my wall.

FAITH TO MOVE A HILL

Great faith to move a mountain
Would surely give a thrill,
But I'd be glad to have
A faith to move some hills.
For hills have slowed me down,
And things I cannot master;
And faith must move them, surely,
If I move forward faster.
Lord, let saints move their mountains!
The one thing that I'm needing
Is faith to deal with hills
That keep me from succeeding.

SOME BLESS THEIR CROSS

Two men on crosses hung
And each man sought release;
One sought release from nails—
The other, inner peace.
One sought escape from shame,
The other turned to Christ;
One asked to be set free,
One begged for Paradise.
One cursed his cross and died—
His life a tragic story;
The other used his cross
To catapult to glory.
Today we each have crosses
That last while life endures;
Some bless their cross, some curse.
What have you done with yours?

IT GLEAMED THROUGH THORNS

A person's greatness can't be hid
But comes in many forms;
Sometimes it comes through sunshine days,
Sometimes it comes through storms.
A person's greatness is revealed
In many, many ways;
Sometimes it shines when we are cursed,
Sometimes it's when we're praised.
A person's greatness will be seen
When fame his name adorns;
Sometimes it comes in other ways;
For Christ it gleamed through thorns.

EARTH IS UNFORGIVING

I'm not afraid to say to life and friends "goodby,"
But that's the coward's wish to exit life and die.
It takes a heart heroic and a mind unafraid
To face life head-long and face it unafraid.
For living isn't simple and earth is unforgiving,
But if it were easy, it wouldn't be worth living.

THESE THINGS I'VE LOVED

I've loved the hills of home,
And on their lofty heights
I've heard daybreak and seen
The day embrace the night.
I've loved the restless tide
Reclining on the shore,
Awaiting dawn to come
To leave with thunderous roar.
I've loved the thunder-clap,
And lightning in the storm,
And beside my window smiled
To see my God perform.

HE NEVER LEARNED HIS NAME

One of my wealthier neighbors recently told me of the merriest Christmas he ever experienced. He said, "One Christmas Eve I locked my office door and started home, feeling the Spirit of Christmas had snubbed me that year. As I left the building on that bitterly cold day I saw on the usual street corner the usual little paper boy shouting the headlines. I, slipping into my warm overcoat, noticed he had no overcoat. The dirty jacket he wore was much too large for his frail shoulders. It was also so thin he shivered with chill. Having purchased papers from him, on an impulse, I invited him to follow me into a nearby department store. To his surprised delight I had him fitted with a fur-lined leather coat. The shining eyes of a grinning boy excited me so I asked him if he owned a bicycle. Upon learning he did not, I accompanied him to the bicycle department and invited him to select the bicycle of his choice. Overcome with gladness, he could hardly decide but finally settled on one of the shiniest and costliest ones. When he saw me paying for it he tossed his papers aside and jumped for joy saying, 'Just what I've been wanting! Just what I've been wanting!'

"Forgetting about his papers, he rode off into the thinning Christmas crowd shouting over his shoulder, 'Thanks! Thanks a lot! Thanks a lot, Mister.' As he disappeared, the smile I had seen wreathed upon his face filled my heart with the true Christmas spirit. I believe that was the little boy's brightest and best Christmas. I know that it was my best one," my neighbor concluded.

"What was the little boy's name?" I asked.

The modest lawyer replied, "Come to think about it, I don't believe I ever asked him his name."

THE CHRIST OF THE GHETTO

"It's awfully dark in here,"
I said to one confined;
"Are you not lonely here
And hungry half the time?"
Her answer startled me
As she lay on her bed;
"Could one be hungry here
When Jesus is his bread?
And though this little room
Is dark without a window,
God's love shines through each crack
And fills my room with splendor."

FIRST IMPRESSIONS

I forgot to notice his handsome face and clothes;
I only remember how loud he blew his nose.
I forgot to notice her furs and costly mink;
I only remember her breath did surely stink.
First impressions count most and help us win
The scorn of foes or the love of friends.

PICKING UP GLASS

Each day a small oil can
He took where'er he went,
And silenced things that squeaked
And never charged a cent.
If in his path he found
Some bits of broken glass,
He picked them up, so girls
And barefoot boys could pass.
Most folk just laughed at him
And yet those golden deeds
Have preached more faith to me
Than all the ancient creeds.

OUR WORLD GETS TOO SMALL

At close of day, kneeling beside his bed, my six-year-old and I were repeating in unison the Lord's Prayer. When we prayed, "Thy Kingdom come," I felt a pat on my shoulder. He whispered, "Dad, let's not pray that part. God's Kingdom has goofed."

At first I thought he was trying to be funny and shock me with his newly acquired, unorthodox language. "Why do you think God's Kingdom has goofed?" I asked.

In simplicity and seriousness he replied, "Because Sammy still cusses and Randy screams and fusses at his Mother. Oh yeah! there's something else, Dad! Gary still hits me and thinks he's big."

Suddenly I realized my little boy's world was hardly bigger than our yard. Certainly it was no bigger than our small town. Of course he had a right to be discouraged about the Kingdom of God with the Sammys, Randys and Garys going about. I tried to tell him the Kingdom of God is greater than our yard, our town, our nation, even bigger than our world. Such explanations fail when you're talking to a six-year-old. Without finishing our prayer, he crawled up into his bed believing what his narrow yard and disappointing playmates forced him to believe.

However, I learned a worthwhile lesson that night. I realized much of my own discouragement and frustration resulted from having too small a world. I, too, had been judging God's kingdom by isolated defeats, incidental happenings and little-hearted people; since then my world has grown and God's coming kingdom has taken on fresh dimensions of greatness.

BECAUSE YOU TALKED TO ME

When I was so in need
Somehow you chanced to call
And you just talked to me
And I felt ten feet tall.
You didn't know my need
Nor could you ever see
The miracle wrought that day
When you just talked to me.
But friend, I felt so brave
When you left me that day
Because you talked to me
And knew just what to say.

EXPERIENCE

I accept the law of gravity and other scientific concepts
Of Newton, Farrady, and others concerning falling objects.
But most of all I believe because I've fallen myself;
I've experienced the law of gravity. How could I not accept?
Likewise, I believe the Bible: a hell, a Christ, a heaven above.
I accept because I've experienced God's Presence, forgiveness and love.

CHRIST'S OTHER WORD

If I had said, "Go fight for faith,"
You would have volunteered,
And if I'd said, "Debate your faith,"
You would have loudly cheered.
If I had said, "Defend your faith,"
You would, no doubt, have done it,
Or even if I'd said, "Go preach,"
You'd doubtless have begun it.
But since I said, "Go live your faith
And live so none can doubt,"
You said, though not in speech or script,
"Lord, you can count me out."

THANKS, MRS. CARRUTHERS

A senior citizen, past eighty, once gave me a poem she composed. It touched me quite deeply. All of it is worthy of printing, but here is a sample.

> "Think not lightly of children's play
> Or the many things they do,
> For their small troubles are to them
> As big as yours are to you.
> And sometimes our greatest pleasures
> And sometimes our sweetest joys
> Come from mending broken playthings
> And broken hearts of girls and boys."
>   —Eva Carruthers

Soon after reading this thought-provoking poem, a knock came on my office door. "Dad," my small son asked, "when are you going to fix my broken bike?"

I'm sure he expected to hear once again, "Perhaps I'll fix it soon. Today I'm just too busy."

However, with the thought of that poem pervading my mind, fixing a broken bike suddenly seemed more important than preparing another sermon. How surprised with joy he became when he heard me say, "Son, let's go and fix it right now. It's been broken long enough."

In a misty rain I bent over that bicycle until darkness fell, remembering what one dedicated parent said, "I'd rather have an aching back today than suffer a broken heart for years to come." My tiredness left as he rode off and shouted over his shoulder, "Thanks, Dad!"

TRUSTING GOD

God calls us not to peace alone
Where joys abide with pains unknown.
God bids us not to dwell always
Where bluebirds sing through sunshine days.
But God calls us to live these years
Trusting Him in spite of fears.
We're called to live a life of trust
Believing God provides for us

GOLDEN ANNIVERSARY PRESENT

With wrinkled, time-worn hands
Half-folded in her lap,
She rocked in her arm chair
And caught an evening nap.
And as she nodded there,
My eyes brimmed full of tears,
But they were tears of thanks
For fifty married years.
Her hands were weary hands,
Pain-wracked with swollen joints,
Yet spools of thread lay there
Beside her needlepoint.
"That's so like her," I thought.
These years had not destroyed
Her lifelong scheme to keep
Her hands always employed.
'Twas then with love and tears
I stooped and touched each hand,
And just as she awoke,
I kissed her wedding band.

THE REAL ISSUE

It's not, "What did you do
With tough breaks and paths blocked?"
The question is what did you do
When opportunity knocked?
It's not whether or not
Curve balls were thrown at you;
The question is, "When strikes whizzed past
What did you bravely do?"
It's not, "Were you shortchanged
Of talents when you started?"
But what have you been doing
With talents God imparted?

THE TASK

When least prepared to choose, young people have to choose
How they will live their lives and how their talents use.
So young and tender they, so grave the choices given,
Yet youth so unprepared choose lives of hell or heaven.
All questions they must answer which life is sure to ask;
How strange when least prepared, God gives the hardest task.

THE COURAGE NOT TO FLEE

I'd rather be a slave
Shackled by my slavery,
Than flee my post of duty
When life demanded bravery.
I'd rather venture not
Than withdraw half-discouraged
From life's great battlefield,
Convinced I lacked true courage.
I'd sooner die ten deaths
At hands of foes empowered,
Rather than live for years
Convinced I was a coward.

WHAT IS A CHRISTIAN?

Frail arms by which Christ lifts,
Weak lips by which He speaks,
A heart through which He loves
And feet by which He seeks.
A soul indwelt by Christ
And eyes through which He sees,
A mind that thinks His thoughts
And hands that strive to please.
A life where Jesus lives,
A will which He commands;
A yielded mind and heart,
Surrendered feet and hands.

ONLY THE GALLANT

None deserves success without a struggle,
And victory is sweetest after a battle.
None deserves happiness who's lived unfaithful,
And none deserves love if he lives ungrateful.
Only the gallant who strives uncomplaining
Deserves the victory of finding life's meaning.

WHAT IS BEAUTY?

I have a friend so young
With handsome face and fair
And there's an elegance
About her golden hair.
I have another friend
Who's lost her youthful grace,
For she's let hands of time
Pinch wrinkles in her face.
But rarer beauty dwells
With her whose hair is streaked,
For I see patience there
And love in wrinkled cheeks.

A MILE THAT SHOWED CONCERN

During the week he was a bus driver. On Sunday he taught our Sunday School class. At fifteen, like many youths, I became a Sunday School dropout. I assured myself, "No one will miss me." How wrong I was. It took me by surprise when Mr. Tisdale knocked on the door of my home. Maybe it was the hurt look in his eyes; maybe it was the concern I saw in his face; perhaps it was the fact he had walked nearly a mile to impress upon me how much I was needed. Whatever it was, it worked miracles. Promises were made. The following Sunday I kept those promises. This happened nearly twenty-five years ago.

Recently, on a Sunday morning, preparing to preach again, I felt a strong urge to write my first letter of appreciation to my old Sunday School teacher. I wrote, "Mr. Tisdale, had you not walked up my dusty road that day and placed your hand on the shoulder of a discouraged boy who needed desperately to know somebody cared, it well may be I would not be a minister today. Thank you very much!"

One week passed and I received a reply. It began, "Your inspired letter came right after a near-fatal heart attack. It was better for me than a doctor's prescription. You see, I've been reviewing my life and wondering if I'd done anything worthwhile. Today I've been greatly encouraged by your letter which I have read and reread. How strange that something I did so long ago and had almost forgotten should bring me such comfort and strength today. How glad and thankful I am that I walked that mile to win you back for the Sunday School. In this hospital room today your letter has brought me unusual joy."

WE MAY CATCH UP WITH HIM

So skeptics fear this age
Has left the Christ behind
And that His ancient thoughts
Insult the modern mind.
Well, I have news for them
Which history long has hinted;
Columns of progress march
Behind bruised feet, nail-printed.
We may catch up with Him
Yet skeptics still will hunt
New ways to update Christ,
Not knowing He's out front.

PEOPLE ARE LIKE TREES

Tall trees sometimes
When storms are lashing,
Groan and surprise us
When we see them crashing.
Those who ask "Why"
Usually learn the truth:
They're rotten inside
Or lack deep roots.

NO VACANCY

Oh God, give me a heart
As great as earth is great;
Yet let in me be found
No room to harbor hate.
Oh God, give me a mind
Vast as this universe;
Yet let there be in me
No room, one grudge to nurse.
Dear God, give me a soul
As spacious as the skies;
Yet may there be in me
No room to shelter lies.

SOME CANDY FOR JESUS' SAKE

One week-end, hitchhiking back to college, I was offered a ride by a man in an expensive, late-model car. That ride and the accompanying conversation have left a lasting impression on me. He, a Roman Catholic businessman, was on his way to a spiritual retreat at a certain monastery. In a cordial fashion we shared our mutual faith and fellowshipped with each other as only Christians may.

When we arrived at his destination, I thanked him and opened the door of the car. It took me by surprise when he offered me a two-pound bag of old-fashioned orange slice candy, which lay on the seat between us.

"Thanks," I said quite curiously. "I really shouldn't." Without a word he reached across the car and pressed the bag of candy into my one empty hand. "I do appreciate this," I said. "But why are you doing it?"

The Catholic layman, whom I had known less than two hours and whom I have never seen since, smiled faintly and spoke kindly, "I am doing this for Jesus' sake." Disarmed by his reply, I knew I must not refuse his gesture of kindness. With my suitcase in one hand and a bag of candy in the other, I stood stunned and speechless as his shiny car turned up a tree-lined street. The rest of that day, hitch-hiking and munching orange-slice candy, I pondered the meaning of his words, "I am doing this for Jesus' sake."

Today those simple words, so fondly recalled, challenge, inspire, reprove, and direct my life. Convinced that only such deeds please Him who died for me, I now seek something to do for Jesus' sake every day.

WAIT LORD

"Thy kingdom come," I prayed
When our small prayer-group met,
But friends knew not I meant,
"Thy kingdom come, but not yet."
"Thy will be done," I prayed
Kneeling beside my mate,
But she knew not I meant,
"Thy will be done, but wait."
"Please use me, Lord," I prayed
When called upon to pray
But class-members knew not
I meant, "Use me, someday."
"Now bless me, Lord," I prayed
While I at church did bow,
And none knew God told me,
"I'll bless you, but not now."

NEUTRALITY

He who can silent stand
When truth is being tried,
Withholding facts he knows,
Afraid to take a side,
Will find he's being judged
By truth confronting him,
And for his coward act
He'll find himself condemned;
Condemned to hell on earth
Deserved and unbegrudged,
Because he silent stood
When truth was being judged.

WHAT WOULD YOU HAVE DONE?

Greatness sometimes goes unnoticed because heroic acts of courageous men are sometimes acted out on obscure stages of life with few to witness the drama. Such may have been the case of one of my good neighbors who's gone to heaven now. I, with only slight knowledge of this long-ago event was able to extract the following story from my reluctant friend:

"Yes, I did run for sheriff of this county at one time. That was a long time ago. I emerged victorious from the first primary and that was the beginning of my ordeal. Disreputable men representing certain illegal businesses in this county approached me concerning specific concessions and compromises they expected of every sheriff, so they could continue their operation outside the law. For such immunity they promised me a pushover election and plenty of revenue—bribe money—once elected."

"What did you say?" I asked.

"Well, what could I say? I'm a Christian. I believe in the Christian way of life," he affirmed.

"But what did you tell them that day?" I asked.

"Nothing," he answered. "I pointed them to the door."

"But what did they say?" I inquired.

"They left threatening that I did not now have a chance in a million at being elected," he responded.

"Then what?" I said.

"My defeat that fall under those circumstances has brought me more satisfaction than any other so-called achievement of my life," he concluded. "It's a pillow of comfort under my aging head."

PRESCRIPTION FOR SELF-PITY

From life's inequities
I pitied my poor self,
But all self-pity fled
When I saw one born deaf.
I wept because I had
To wear eye-glasses thick,
But when a blind man passed
I felt ashamed and sick.
I crippled on a crutch
And grieved from night 'til dawn,
But weeping ceased when I
Saw one with both legs gone.

IF I MUST SEE FAULTS

I see my neighbors faults and errors of my friends
But I am unaware of my besetting sins.
How strange I can't see them, but of my virtues though,
I'm much aware and proud, should any care to know.
Lord, help me see the goodness of friends I've loved and known,
And if I must see faults, please let them be my own.

A MUSTARD SEED FAITH

The flimsiest faith is enough
If placed in Christ the Lord,
But the strongest faith is vain
If not based on God's word.
Great faith if misdirected
Cannot secure God's favor,
But shabbiest faith can save
A soul who trusts the Savior.
Then faith need not be strong
To meet a person's needs;
Christ praised a child-like faith,
As small as mustard seeds.

DENOMINATIONS DIVIDE

To quote the same creed
And read the same Bible
And repeat the same prayer
Christ taught His disciples,
Should unify Christians
And help them find favor
In each other's eyes
Who love the same Savior.
But our two churches
On opposite sides of the street
Hardly know each other
Or speak when we meet.
Denominations divide
And sadly bother
Getting together with others
Who love the same Father.

RETRIBUTION

I said to myself, "My wild oats I'll scatter;
It's nobody's business. My deeds don't matter."
For every thrill I had, a hundred tears I weep;
Each seed of sin I sowed, a hundred-fold I reap.

VACATIONS BLESS

Breathless I scanned vast plains
Without one home in sight,
Glimpsed snow-capped peaks, moonlit,
Punching holes in night.
I gazed at nude seashores
Lusting after trees,
Scaled cliffs of white limestone
Embraced by loveless seas.
Yet when bleak wintertime
Barricaded spring
Shut-in, 1 found delight
Recounting breathless things.

AS GOOD AS TRUTH

Love America? You bet
Pray tell, why not?
Can you tell me where there's
A fairer spot?
Love America? I'll say!
Can one do less,
And then in prayer ask God
His land to bless?
Love America? Indeed.
And I from tender youth
Have loved her next to God
And good as truth.

MY BEGINNING

Today is to my past a day of ending,
But to the rest of my life, today is the beginning.
What though my past is marred, or my task unfinished?
Today I'll start all over with a future unblemished.
Today I'll change my pace from failure to winning,
Because to the rest of my life, today is my beginning.

AFTER THOUGHTS

I passed him on the road
As I drove into town
And I half-way knew him
Who walked so burdened down.
I felt I should have stopped
But being in a hurry
I turned my head and passed
Saying, "That's not my worry."
But Christian that I am
(At least I claim to be)
Can't help but wonder what
He thinks of God and me.

HOW TO GET WHAT YOU WANT

When an eight-year-old son announces that he expects drums for Christmas what do you say? After his parents had discussed it privately, we announced the sad news. No drums! Our son accepted it like a good soldier but not without re-stating his wish. Whether planned or not, his tactic was to find new ways of expressing the deep desire of his heart. From the first week of November through December, we heard it in a variety of ways —drums, drums, drums. We discouraged his dream, or attempted to, but still he offered the tender request, "But I want drums!"

One week before Christmas we decorated our tree and one of the first gifts to be placed under the tree was marked *GUESS WHO!*, and it was big enough to contain drums, at least our child thought so. He at first whispered it to his brothers and then to his parents and finally to every child in the community, "My drums are under the Christmas tree."

He even went so far as to thank us saying, "I knew I would get those drums. Thanks!" The more we tried to convince him otherwise the more he would reply, "I know you're just saying that. That box is for me and it's my drums." His childish faith broke down his parents' will.

On Christmas Eve I made a special trip to a nearby city. Upon returning, my car contained a very special thing, a large box of gift-wrapped drums. On Christmas morning it was worth it all. Disappointed with the *GUESS WHO* box, he found his dream answered as he opened the second big box with his name on it. His faith, his faith *alone*, achieved the impossible! Is not that how prayer works? God is looking today for someone who has the faith of a little child. Will you be that one?

SILENT THINGS

Let me remember silent things,
Remembered from my childhood springs;
Slow melting snow on sun-splashed peaks,
Mute trees that try with buds to speak,
And spring-time sun that gently goes
As silent as it first arose.
Let me remember silent things
Like winter's rosy fireside scenes,
And snow, fresh-fallen, soft and deep
That charmed us 'til we fell asleep,
And silent trees all caked with snow
Like saints at prayer with heads bowed low.
If I recall these silent things
It matters not what my life brings.
In woe I'm sure I'll stand steadfast
And win my cherished goal at last,
To be an isle of peace and poise,
Amidst life's sea of strife and noise.

TAKE UP YOUR CROSS

I said, "You ask too much!
A fellow has to live;
Still You come begging me
To give and give and give."
"And do I ask too much?
And does one have to live?
I had to die," He wept,
"And pray, 'Forgive, forgive.'"

A PLACE FOR STARTING OVER

One thing above all things
I wish that I could find,
A place for starting over
The land of being kind.
A cross to crucify
My spirit too demanding,
A spot to leave behind
Each harsh misunderstanding,
That I might start anew,
And yet each dawn, somehow,
I hear my Master whisper,
"The time and place is now."

THE END PRODUCT

I know as a parent I have my choice
Of being more agreeable and softening my voice,
'Til I, undemanding, am praised unending
By children untaught who lack understanding.
But forfeiting popularity to enforce discipline,
I know in the end I'll raise good citizens.

CHURCH WORK

The nicest words I've ever heard
Came when my preacher asked,
"For Jesus and His church would you
Perform a special task?"
Surprised my church should think of me,
I said that I would do it,
Especially since I'd craved church work
Though not a person knew it.
Through all these years that memory shines
And means so very much—
The day the preacher gave to me
A special task at church.

GOD REMEMBERS

I placed them here, crisp bulbs so brown,
And shoved them deep into the ground.
In haste I failed to mark the spot
And as days passed I soon forgot.
But I, surprised, when weeks marched by,
Saw tulips growing half knee-high.
I guess God marks bulbs planned for spring;
It's great how He remembers things.

TO SQUEEZE THY GLORY OUT

In youth and in old age, in pleasure and in strife,
Lord, help me do Thy will, get glory from my life.
And if I half-forgetful, put not Thy kingdom first,
And if for righteousness I lose my deeper thirst,
Then Lord, in hot displeasure, purge me from fear and doubt,
And crush me if it's needed to squeeze Thy glory out.

WE OUGHT TO GET THEM BACK

Our old smokehouse that use to be
Exists no more for eye to see.
Smokehouses went like one-room schools
And turning-plows hitched up to mules.
We ought to get smokehouses back,
Smoke seeping out of every crack;
But they went out like fires we fixed
Of hickory chips and sassafras sticks.
Yet still I see in my mind's eye
Smokehouses filled with hams hung high.
And smell again the fragrance good—
Smoke rising from ham-smoking wood.

SPEAK UP WITH COURAGE

When Martin Luther cried,
"God help me, Here I stand!"
He struck a note for freedom
That rung across the land.
When brave Columbus roared
To mutiny-minded seamen,
"Sail on! I say, sail on!"
He rang the bell of freedom.
When Patrick Henry shouted,
"Give me liberty or death,"
He strengthened freedom's cause
With that courageous breath.
When brave McArthur wept
And vowed, "I will return,"
He wrote a page for freedom
Which all the world must learn.
Since freedom is never free
Let us say when discouraged,
"As millions have died for freedom
Let us speak up with courage."

A DELINQUENT'S PLEA

The judge said, "Son, I know
Your dad of wealth and fame,
And now I must inquire
Why you've disgraced his name?"
The boy replied, "I've thought
A lot since I've been jailed,
And if I've failed him, Sir,
It's first, because he failed.
Back when I needed him
He'd say 'I'm busy, lad,
And though he's famed and rich,
He failed me as a dad."

CLOSED CHAPTERS

When he marched off to school
I knew I had no choice,
But afterthoughts left me
Unable to rejoice.
And though I kissed his cheek,
Yet how could I be glad?
For he was only six—
The last small child I had.
'Twas then I sensed somehow,
As I waved to my son,
A chapter in life's book
For me was nearly done.

HEARTBREAK AT DAWN

Exhibiting indifference and displaying immunity
To the patient knocking of opportunity,
And even refusing, when hearing the knock,
To turn the key quickly and unlock the lock,
Is the curse of today and the heartbreak at dawn
To discover tomorrow—opportunity has gone.

HOW GOD WORKS

I begged my God to give
To me a sincere friend,
But He gave love and said,
"Each one His own must win."
I dreamed a dream and prayed
That world-wide strife would cease
But God touched my weak voice
And said, "You speak for peace."
When I prayed, "Smooth my path;
Replace my dingy hovel;"
God only gave me tools—
A hammer, saw and shovel.

TO SHARE A WORLD OF LOVE

I've never been abroad
Or spanned the spacious seas,
Or scaled the mountains tall
Or felt the Arctic freeze.
But here in childhood paths
With home scenes loved so dear,
Fate has decreed it seems
That I should linger near.
What though I am denied
Luxury, wealth or ease?
I think of me as blest
And wealthy if you please.
I've known the love of children;
I've had a loyal wife;
I've loved my neighbors dearly;
I've tasted deep of life.
To share a world of love
Makes me not feel offended
That I've not been abroad;
My narrow world is splendid.

FOR WE'VE SEEN OUR BRAVE PARENTS

Let us so live our lives
In these dark desperate days
That children in our homes
Will sense we're strong and brave.
Let us conduct ourselves
On this and every day
In such courageous fashion
'Til children of us say,
"God matched us with the future
And made us fearless of it,
For we've seen our grave parents
Face their trouble and solve it."

WHAT ARE WE HERE FOR

What are we here for? Not to gather wealth,
Or capture great fame, or enjoy health.
We're here for one thing—and that's to help each other,
To heal some broken hearts, to lift a fallen brother.
And these are all our brothers, and they are all in need,
And we're here to help them—in words and gifts and deeds.

TO FORGIVE IS TO FORGET

I said, "I will forgive
But I can ne'er forget,"
And I heard whispered words
Which I remember yet.
"Did God forgive your sins
And still remember them?"
With shame I dropped my head
As I replied to Him,
"Of course, the Lord forgets
When He forgives, it's true."
"Then go," He said, "forgive
As I've forgiven you."

THOUGHTS FROM THE SLUMS

Shivering boys passed a church
And one waif asked, "What's that?"
The other said, "A church
Where Christians worship at."
"Then let's go in," he cried;
"It looks so warm in there."
"No! no!" the other said,
"They're having songs and prayer.
Besides," the urchin said,
"Church-folk don't seem to be
Too much concerned about
Poor kids like you and me."

WE CAN CONQUER DEATH

God has not promised
Us perfect health,
Glory and glomour,
Or limitless wealth.
God has not promised
Exemption from
Aches and agony
When illness comes.
But God has promised
His strength will brighten
Our golden years
When shadows lengthen.
And God has promised
Throughout life's days
Goodness and mercy
Shall follow always.

OUR WORK IS PLANNED

God has not promised
A task untiring,
A pleasant place
With work inspiring.
God has not promised
A life of ease
Where work delights
And people please.
But God has promised
That every man
Has a task assigned
Like a blue-print plan.
And He has promised
Time is extended
For each to finish
Work God intended.

I KNOW NOW

My mother never slept
No matter where we'd been
Until she knew for sure
Her children were all in.
We'd beg her not to wait
But she could not refrain,
And when we asked her "Why?"
She never could explain.
But since I have some girls
And sons as tall as men,
I know how Mother felt
Until we all came in.

HALF AS GREAT

Your boast of family ties and your ancestors blest,
Nauseates me slightly. Frankly, I'm unimpressed.
Ancestors of which you brag—brave-hearted and self-giving,
Suggest your kin, somehow, are better dead than living.
I doubt your kinsmen's fame and even their fate
Unless, alive, you produce posterity half as great.

CHILDREN REMEMBER

The pleasures that you give
To boys and girls today
Will bring them happiness
When years have passed away.
For kindly words you speak
And loving deeds you do
Will warm their hearts for years
And they'll remember you.
But break one childish heart,
And when that child is grown
He'll not forget your name
Though fifty years have flown.

WHEN THE CHURCH PRAYS

A burden lifted from his heart,
A load he could not bear,
Yet he knew not back home his church
Was remembering him in prayer.
She sensed the uplift hope inspires,
And strong faith made her merry,
But she knew not her church was praying
For her, its missionary.
Grief-stricken by his first-born's grave,
He heard the Master saying,
"Be strong!"—But he knew not back home
His church for him was praying.
When dark clouds lift and light breaks through
We're usually unaware
That someone back home who loves us
Has called our name in prayer

GOD LOVES US AS WE ARE

You don't have to make home runs
When you stand up to bat;
Just try to get on first base
Or a little better than that.
You don't have to make it big
From your business earnings;
Just try to make a good living
And keep the home fires burning.
And you don't have to be famous
With a much-praised name;
Faithfulness in small things is better
Than making halls of fame.
If you can't be the sun or moon,
Settle for the evening star;
We don't have to prove our greatness.
God loves us as we are.

JUST REHEARSING

May it be said of me
When I bow from life's stage,
"He played with all his heart
The role he should have played."
May it be said of me
When life's last curtains fall,
"He played his part with zest
Although his part was small."
And may I hear God say
When from the stage I bow,
"Rehearsal days are done;
Your starring role starts now."

SCARS

No nail-scars mark my feet; I never knew such losses;
But I for love of Jesus, am foot-sore bearing crosses.
No nail-prints scar my hands; I never knew such malice;
But I in serving Jesus, have hands work-worn and calloused.
No sword has pierced my heart; such crime I can't perceive;
But I for grief He bore, have broken-hearted, grieved.

THE VISITOR

For years each day at six a.m.
He went to church and bowed his knee
And meekly prayed, "Dear God, it's Jim."
And when he'd leave we all could see
The Presence came and walked with him.
As Jim grew old the chastening rod
Of years left him so ill and drawn
His path to church is now untrod;
But in his room each day at dawn
He hears a voice, "Dear Jim, it's God!"

WHERE GOD IS FOUND

God is more often found
Where hearts are crushed with grief
Than in cold stuffy churches
Where sermonettes are preached.
God is more likely known
Through lives of gentle people
Than through stain-glassed cathedrals
Adorned with cross-tipped steeple.
God is much clearer seen
Where souls with crosses falter
Than from new pews upholstered
Encircling ivory altars

WE'D LAUGH

If Christ should come once more to live among us men,
I think we'd treat Him kinder than Pharisees back then.
I think we'd ask Him home, inviting Him for dinner,
And treat Him like a guest instead of some vile sinner.
We're much more civil now. Yet soon as we were fed
We'd talk 'til He departed, then laugh at what He said.

TO WITNESS WITH LIFE

You never mentioned faith
And yet I say sincerely,
I have a stronger faith.
Your life has witnessed clearly.
You never mentioned kindness
And yet in some strange fashion
You've witnessed with your life
Of Christ and His compassion.
You never mentioned Jesus,
Yet I in spiritual blindness
Have found my sight restored,
And Christ revealed through kindness.

THE SILENT FOLK

The deeper streams in silence flow,
While shallow brooks still babble;
Full ships sink low and empty cars
On railroad tracks still rattle.
The silent folk like silent stars
On darkest nights shine best,
And burdened hearts like ships bowed down
Are still the ones that bless

EARTH MUST CHOOSE BROTHERHOOD

Hats off to modern science
And scientists wise and good,
For through their skill the world
Became a neighborhood.
Science made the far-off lands
Seem like they're at our door,
And super-sonic planes
Will shrink the world much more.
Science made a neighborhood;
One choice confronts us still:
Earth must choose brotherhood
Or be a battlefield.

DEEPER ROOTS

Tree roots grow deeper still
And take on stronger form
When trees are lashed by winds
And bruised by freezing storms.
Like trees that deeper grow
By straining in the sod,
I, too, bowed low, sank roots
Deep in the heart of God

47

PETER'S REMORSE

Some think Peter's remorse
For cowardice he showed,
Caused him through life to kneel
And weep when roosters crowed.
And yet this seems opposed
To truth the scriptures teach;
When roosters crowed at dawn,
I think he rose to preach.

YOU CAN CHANGE THE WORLD

If you can walk with head held high
And look men squarely in the eye,
Nor stoop to steal or tell a lie,
Then you can change the world.
If you can sit with men condemned
Nor feel you are too good for them
But witness to His cross and Him,
Then you can change the world.
And with the love which Christ imparted
If you can rise when day has started
Stoop down to lift the broken-hearted,
Then you can change the world.

IF YOU'LL ONLY LISTEN

In November please remember
When the weather grows chilled,
Many poor children starve,
Shivering and ill.
In December please remember
When lights of Christmas glisten,
Children can be heard crying
If you'll only listen.

BALANCING THE BOOK

When saddened by slow progress
I think of where I'm from,
Of obstacles surmounted
And just how far I've come.
When failures dog my steps
And tasks face me half-finished,
I re-count victories won
And pleasures undiminished.
When from my poor performance
Remorse is unrelieved,
I balance my book of failures
With triumphs I've achieved.

AS A STRANGER

Today a stranger attendèd church but since none knew him,
And since we were busy worshipping, nobody welcomed him.
Cold-hearted we come to church, cold-hearted we left the same,
Ignoring the stranger completely; nobody knew his name.
"I missed Christ presence at worship," I cried.
He wept, "As a stranger I came but no one recognized."

IN RETROSPECT

The irony of my life
Is that my earthly days
Have all been spent going
Unknown, unchosen ways,
And doing work which I
Had never planned to do,
And living in some towns
Of which I never knew.
Yet, strangely, life thus lived
Need not be life misspent,
For mine in retrospect
Seems like the life God meant.

BRIDGE BUILDING

If I my work could choose
I'd ask the all-wise Giver
To let me build a bridge
Across some angry river.
Or else tear down some wall
Where neighbors used to walk,
And then I'd clear a path
So they could meet and talk.
For that's the greatest work
And that is why I'd rather
Blast walls and build bridges,
So friends could get together.

I MET HIM IN DEPTH

As I look back on life
I'm sure I did not know
My God in deeper ways
'Til illness brought me low.
At last I met Him there
In ways I'd never known.
My illness taught me how
To trust in Him alone.
In casual ways I knew
My God across the years,
But I met Him in depth
Through illness, grief, and tears.

I'D RATHER BE A PAGAN

I'd rather be a heathen with understanding dim
Than live where Christ is worshipped and not worship Him.
I'd rather be a pagan or else an infidel,
Than know Christ conquered death, and live as if He failed.
I'd rather never join the church and be baptized
Than be a faithful member and still not know the Christ.

WHEN MEN STAND UP

Let strong men stand for Christ
And let wives follow them,
And then their children challenged
Will also stand for Him.
Let strong men stand for Christ
And boys and girls impressed
Will follow in their steps.
They follow men the best.
Let strong men stand for Christ
If we would save our youth
From sensual, selfish paths,
For Christ, the Way and Truth.

⚜

IF JESUS CAME

If Jesus came to our small town,
He would not wear a robe or gown;
He would not have long hair or beard
Or dress Himself in sandals weird.
He would not have that ancient look
As He appears in picture book;
And if He ever stood to teach
We'd hear no accent in His speech.
I think He'd look like every man,
And seeing Him we'd understand
How if He came to our small town
The people here would turn Him down.
And is that not the reason why
The angry crowds cried, "Crucify!"
The reason they rejected Him
Was that He looked so much like them.
But down our streets as He once came
He comes to us and calls our names;
But we don't know Him in our town.
We wanted Him to wear a crown.

WISE INVESTMENT

Wealth invested in fashions
Will last a year or two;
Wealth invested in education
Will last the whole life through;
Wealth invested in children
Will outlast history's pages,
While wealth spent for God's cause
Will outlast endless ages

A HOME-TOWN WITNESS

Desiring to witness
I volunteered to preach,
But Jesus said to me,
"Go witness on your street."
"I seek a larger place,"
I pled in bold self-pity;
"Then go," He whispered low,
"Go witness in your city."
"I mean elsewhere," I begged,
"Like some far-distant place;
Lord, here in my hometown
They'd laugh right in my face."
He wept, "But Judea mocked;
Galilee turned me down;
Jerusalem spit on me;
They laughed in my home-town."
Deeply touched, I went forth
To witness to my neighbor
Who welcomed and made me glad
I dared to go and labor.
And I, surprised, soon learned
There are no distant places
With needs more deeply etched
Than on familiar faces

WHERE I SAW GOD

Today I saw a man
Freezing in a storm
And I gave him my coat
And made him very warm.
Today I saw a child
Begging on a street
And I gave him a coin
That he might buy and eat.
I saw my God today
But not in usual form;
I saw Him in a child
And met Him in a storm.

TALKING TO THE SHEPHERD

Insomniac I am, have learned the key to sleep
Is talking to my Shepherd instead of counting sheep.
For oft in telling Jesus my fears and doubts and woes
I've found to my delight my sleepless eyes soon close.
Why should I count sheep now when sleepless hours mock?
I've learned to count my blessings and with my Shepherd talk.

WE'RE GOD'S MASTERPIECE

What if some artist took
His greatest work of art
And cut it all to shreds
Destroying every part?
What if some sculptor hauled
His masterpiece in stone
Out to some garbage dump
And left it there alone.
How hardly then can God
From His wise presence fling
The masterpiece of Man
Or crush a treasured thing.

WE NEED ACQUAINTANCESHIP

Does faith mean mouthing creeds
Because they're very old,
Or quoting ancient scripture
Inscribed on ancient scrolls?
Does faith mean facts believed
Which history can't confirm,
Or gulping dogmas down
Which conscience can't affirm?
But surely faith is more
Than trust in facts of history,
Or giving mental nods
To miracles clothed with mystery.
We need the Christian Scriptures
And none should call them odd,
But we need Christian experience,
A first-hand knowledge of God.
We need acquaintanceship
With God in such a way
That knowledge of Him is
More than merely hearsay
Such faith for most of us,
Alas, is too high priced.
Quoting creeds is much easier
Than following Christ

MY CHILDREN

I loved them so when they were small
And kissed each bruise when they would fall.
Their childish feet as day would close
Ofttimes would stand upon my toes.
Around me now no children play,
No feet walk on my toes today.
For since they're grown and live apart,
They only walk upon my heart.

ONE LASTING MEMORIAL

Within these walls of time
And by God's strength and help,
Each one must carve from life
A statue of himself.
Soon we'll be through and gone
And friends, bereft, will grieve,
But a statue of our lives
We'll be required to leave.
So let us chisel here,
With every act of duty,
A masterpiece of art,
A shrine to truth and beauty.

LET NONE STOOP SO LOW

When he speaks ill of others and shreds them right and left,
He doesn't suspect we know he's bragging on himself.
Yet words of gossip kill without pain or compunction
To him who does the killing; that's how a gossip functions.
Then let none stoop so low to speak ill words of others,
If in promoting self we have to hurt our brothers.

THE NEAREST THING TO HEAVEN

Home is the place we turn
At closing of the day,
Where fellowship restores
The strength that's drained away.
Home is the spot we seek
With love that fonder grows,
For friends wait there we love
And we are loved by those.
Home is a reverent place
That grows each year more reverend—
The dearest place on earth,
The nearest thing to heaven.

I DON'T KNOW WHO I AM

Who am I? I'm a zoo!
An eagle soaring high,
A bat, a mole, an ox,
A lion that makes things die.
Oft I'm a wily fox
Deceiving those I like,
Sometimes I am a dove,
Sometimes a snake that strikes.
What a menagerie am I;
I don't know who I am;
Sometimes I run with rabbits;
Sometimes I hunt with hounds.

THE DIVINE PLOWMAN

When plowmen sink their plows
Into a fertile field,
They feel assured there'll be
A fruitful harvest yield.
God is a plowman, too,
And we each one must trust
He has a hope for harvest
When He plows deep on us.
Then let us let Him plow,
Assured from us He'll reap,
And sure we'll soon see why
He plowed on us so deep

HIS GREATNESS WAS HIS WORK

One passion strong possesses me
And grips me in its power
And grows in great intensity
With every passing hour.
For I'm aware when I depart
One question will be asked:
"Did he do well his work assigned
Or piddle at the task?"
One passion strong possesses me
And from it I'll not shirk,
That friends may say when I am gone,
"His greatness was his work."

THE WORLD GOES ON WITHOUT US

Just yesterday I shopped
For groceries here as usual;
Today the door is locked
But it's a kind refusal.
Beneath the wreath it says,
"Last night of heart attack
The owner passed away";
Lord! what a tragic fact!
Such wreaths always surprise,
But it's a kind refusal
For underneath it reads,
"Business tomorrow as usual."

LIFE PAYS US WHAT WE ASK

When some promotion fails
And strife's harsh winds are brewing
We seldom blame ourselves,
But friends for our undoing.
Yet blaming other people
For our defeats and errors
Can't hide the fact we make
Our fears, our hates, our terrors.
Each makes his hell or heaven
According to his goal.
Life pays us what we earn.
We cannot blame a soul.

PEARLS OF WISDOM

In ancient times they say
Pearl-divers were required
To cling to heavy rocks
And dive to depths desired.
They say gigantic stones
Would pull the diver down
So he could search and find
Where costly pearls were found.
Sometimes harsh loads in life,
Like stones, crush with despair
'Til we, submerged in troubles,
Find pearls of wisdom there.

I CAUGHT YOUR FAITH

I saw you stand steadfast in grief
But saw no trace of unbelief.
I saw you stand unmoved by stress
But saw no trace of bitterness.
I saw you stand bravely for years
But saw no trace of senseless fears.
Though you spoke not of faith's firm law,
I caught your faith by things I saw.

BEAUTY, ART AND PLEASURE

I thought life should consist
Of mostly art and pleasure,
But life gave sorrow's cup
And I drank without measure.
I thought life should consist
Of mostly art and beauty,
But life gave work and sweat
And I found life was duty.
Yet duty's rich reward
And sorrow's rarest treasure,
I've learned through toil and tears,
Are beauty, art, and pleasure.

WAITING AT THE GATE

When I came home from work
I'd see him by the gate,
For just at sunset time
My little boy would wait.
I always scooped him up,
His cheek against my cheek,
And oft I pressed a kiss
On one too thrilled to speak.
But my small boy grew tall
And marks of manhood bore,
And boyhood years took flight
To come back nevermore.
Now by that gate I see
No more my little man,
And yet I'm sure it's all
A part of God's great plan.
Yet I'd give all I have
To meet my boy again,
Waiting at the gate
When weary workdays end.

THE BEGINNING OF SERVICE

He came to the church entrance
And whispered to a friend,
"I've come to get my wife;
Has the service come to an end?"
"The worship is nearly over,"
The usher whispered, grinning,
"But the service you speak of
Is just beginning."

PROUD TO STAND BY HIM

The preacher urged his church
When all his words were through,
"Go stand by some aged friend
Who's meant the most to you."
They passed the rich and great
As many took their stand
By one who seldom spoke,
An obscure, older man.
But he in winsome ways
Had shared his faith with them,
And they in gratitude
Were proud to stand by him.

GO GET THEM BACK

Don't let your dreams take flight
For everybody knows
Dreams are the stuff from which
Great deeds and goodness flow.
Don't let your dreams take flight
Or let one dream grow cold,
For when your dreams have died
You've pre-condemned your soul.
Don't let your dreams take flight.
Losing one dream is sin;
And if your dreams have fled
Go get them back again.

SECRETS OF SOLITUDE

Instead of loneliness
When lonely years are viewed,
Great souls term aloneness
As a blest solitude.
Such ones are seldom lonely
And drink so deep of gladness
That aloneness is for them
An exemption from sadness.
And they look back remembering
The thrill of being alone,
And call it solitude
When lonely days have flown.
Secrets of solitude
Dear Lord I'd learn from Thee,
Who fasted for forty days
And braved Gethsemane

A SOUL CONVERTING STATION

Show me a church where people meet
And everyone is friendly,
And one where well-loved scripture verses
Are quoted in sincerity;
And show to me a sanctuary
Where families bow on Sunday,
And where they leave to live that way
When they're at work on Monday;
And I'll show you a growing church,
And without hesitation
A church where lives are changed by Christ,
A soul-converting station.

HEREDITY

Old Grumpy married Sour-puss
And had some little grouches,
And Touch-me-not wed Sorehead's boy
And raised some little ouches.
Old Fatso's girl wed Five-by-five
And had a little blimp
And Two-face married Double-talk
And raised the devil's imp.
Of course the point is plain and clear
Nor need we look too far;
Each child reflects in his own way
Just what his parents are

ENVIRONMENT

Grouch was the family name;
Grim was the oldest brother,
And Greed and Gripe were twins;
Grump was their name for mother.
Beside them lived the Spats
Whose sons were Spit and Spite;
The girls were Sass and Stew
And how they loved to fight.
They lived in Peevish town
(To live there I would waiver)
For Grouches hate the Spats
And Spats return the favor

MOUNTAIN MEN

The finest wood that's known
To make a violin
Is carved from mountain **trees,**
Grown where the air is thin.
For music that exudes
From such violins, we know,
Is lofty as tall peaks,
And sweet as purest snow.
As it is true of trees
So it's with mountain men,
They grow in strength through storms
And facing lashing wind.
Let me, whipped by life's storms,
Pause daily to remember
That best violins are carved
From tested mountain timber.

PEOPLE NEED PRAISE

If at my door I struck
Some beggar's body frail,
I think the law should come
And cart me off to jail.
Yet there's no law against
My crushing someone's mind,
Or letting one starve for
Praises sincere and kind.
Yet praise we oft withhold
From some deserving friend
Is ten times worse, I think,
Than striking beggar men.

SILENT WAYS

It comforts me when I recall
How quietly turns this earthly ball,
For 'midst the noise of man-made violence
God does his work in perfect silence.
How silently sunrises come
And night slips in serenely dumb.
Springtime tiptoes as if it fears
One soul should know when it appears.
And since quiet work brings God high praise
We too must work in silent ways

IT'S GOOD BECAUSE IT'S HIS

God squanders not one thing
Of leaves or sun or frost,
For in His plan no twig
Or sprig of grass is lost.
And in His plan I know
No soul is made in vain,
Although for me at times
His purpose is not plain.
But I shall know someday
Just what His purpose is,
And in the meantime trust
It's good because it's His.

I PROCEED WITH JOY

When I could not go on
Or bear my burdens longer,
Christ stooped to share my load
And made my shoulders stronger.
My trudging feet He touched
Until like feathers light,
I skipped for joy and danced
Along a pathway bright.
His touching me transformed
My cross to silver wings
And I, no longer lonely
Proceed with joy Christ brings.

LET FAITH SHINE BRIGHTER

When trouble seems to double
You still can be courageous,
And courage thus displayed
Proves to be contagious.
When everything goes wrong,
You can still be great-hearted,
And such an attitude
Always helps get things started.
When friends betray and scorn,
You can live such a life
That faith will shine still brighter,
And love extinguish strife.

REMORSE

With heart sincere and steady stroke
I carved my name upon an oak.
'Twas then I vowed to keep my name
Untarnished and exempt from shame.
But as years passed I then realized
My vow to God was compromised.
Yet every promise that I broke
Still haunts me when I pass that oak.

NO LAWLESS SOUL AM I

I scorn the hypocrite
And hate his deeds of sham,
So I in shame condemn
The person that I am.
Sometimes I'm forced to face
My own besetting sin
Aware I've welcomed it
And cherished it within.
No lawless soul am I!
It's just that I can't stand
What I've become at last
In light of what I planned.

STANDING UP TO LIFE

Don't run away and hide
From troubles that you see.
You'll multiply the woes
From which you try to flee.
We ought to meet our troubles
Head-on and unafraid;
It makes our courage grow
And helps our fears to fade.
And if we dauntless face
The frightful, dreaded foe,
We'll find by being brave
Our courage starts to grow;
And soon discover, too,
By standing up to life
That every trouble conquered
Equips for future strife.
Yet if you should forget
And fearful run away,
You'll find, unsolved, each woe
Will seek you out one day.

REMEMBERING GOOD DAYS

Tell of the woes you've missed;
Tell not of pains you've borne;
Tell of the good days spent
But not of days forlorn.
For thoughts of happy days
Will prove to be refreshing,
And wise, indeed, is he
Who daily counts his blessings.
Tell not of dismal days
In pessimistic tone;
Great strength rewards those who
Recount good days they've known.

ONE FEAR

I met an ancient man
With weary steps and slow;
I asked him where he'd been
And where he planned to go.
"I've been in life's great war,"
I heard the man reply,
"And dauntless I go forth
To battle till I die."
"Have you no fear?" I asked.
He said, "I'm fear-possessed
That I will flee my post
When Duty asks my best."

IF I HAD KNOWN

If I had only known
The burden that you bore
I would have taken time
To knock upon your door,
Or I'd have cheered you up
When on a busy street
Your path and mine today
Did accidentally meet.
Tonight I'm sad for words
I was too dumb to say
When you had such a need
And I was blind today.

CREED FOR YOUTH

Go venture life upon a dream,
Reach for the stars, follow the gleam;
Cling to your hopes by faith's surmise,
Walk with your head high in the skies.
And don't forget to venture all
When courage beckons and duty calls.
And give to life all you possess
When it requires your very best.
For soon you'll learn that he who lives
Is only he who truly gives
Of self and love and sacrifice
That's why it pays to follow Christ.

HE'LL MAKE TOMORROW GOOD

Why should I be afraid
Of what the future holds,
For through these years I've found
God's will each day unfolds.
And as I've lived today
With faith that conquers fears
So I will face tomorrow
And future untried years.
I'll fearless face the future
Persuaded and assured
That God of yesteryears
Will make tomorrow good.

IT WAS YOU

Who nailed Him high against the sky?
Who watched Him die as He prayed, "Why?"
It was I! It was I! It was I!
Who hung the Jew in public view
And bruised Him blue and cursed Him too?
It was you! It was you! It was you!
Who mocked His plea, when on the tree
As blood flowed free, He prayed for me?
It was I! It was you! It was we!

A CHRIST-LIKE GOD

Who knows what God is like?
My concept is quite dim;
And yet in Christ I think
I've caught a glimpse of Him.
Who comprehends God's love?
Perhaps the very smart;
And yet in Christ I think
I've glimpsed God's loving heart.
Who understands God's ways
Or where His feet have trod?
Yet I through Christ perceive
He is a Christ-like God

HIS MESSAGE THRIVES

No news photographers
Recorded on a film
The crucifixion scene
And what they did to Him.
No news reporters wrote
On scroll or ancient chart
How spikes and spears were used
To stop His broken heart.
But that the world may know
Of love He had for them
He sent them forth to share
And they went preaching Him.
Two thousand years have fled
And still His message thrives,
For Jesus writes His love
On human hearts and lives.

THE PRINCIPLE OF FAITH

If you are one of those
Who have a faith implicit
In some good doctor's skill,
Then you've learned faith's top secret.
If you in frantic need
Have sought out your physician,
And left with fears relieved,
Then you know faith's conditions.
If you've risked life and limb
To some great surgeon's skill,
Then you could be a saint
With faith in God as real.

HE'S REAL TO ME

I've never heard His voice
Nor glimpsed His face so wise
Or gripped His nail-torn hand
Or gazed into His eyes.
Yet echoes of His voice
I've heard above the storm
And oft at worship time
I've glimpsed His shadowed form.
His robe I've never touched
Or heard Him call my name,
Yet He's more real to me
Than any friend I claim

THE MAN I OUGHT TO BE

Struggling deep within
Demanding to be free
Is one I hardly know,
The man I ought to be
Too long I've chained him down
With chains of greed and lust!
Too long I've left him bound
With deeds and words unjust.
Thou man I ought to be,
Too long I've heard you cry;
God, help me free at last
The good man that is I.

LIFE IS A STORY BOOK

Life is a story book
And with the dawning light
God gives to each of us
A clean new page to write.
Each year a chapter ends
And all we've written there
Can never be erased,
So let us write with care.
Then write great words and deeds,
Not hate or theft or bribery,
That all we write may be
Fit for heaven's great library

SO LET ME DIE IN FAITH

My body weary from these years
Will to the earth return,
But my soul freed from flesh will soar
To God for whom I yearn.
And friends will do me wrong to say
I'm buried in a tomb
Or weep beside my grave not knowing
I'm in my Father's room.
Set free by death, my soul can't be
Imprisoned in a grave;
When breath expires my soul will fly
Back to the God who gave.
What seems like death to fearful men,
Let me reach to embrace,
Convinced that Christ will be there waiting.
So let me die in faith!

YET I THINK MARY WEPT

Who would have ever guessed
The God who made the world
Would one day enter it
Born of a peasant girl?
And that upon her breast
The God who reigns above
Would there enrobed in flesh
Reveal the Father's love?
Yet I think Mary wept
When flames of candles tossed
Rude shadows in the stall—
And she could see a cross

I ROSE TO BROTHER ALL

When I once prayed, "Our Father,"
My tears I could not hide.
That day, for the first time
I saw what it implied.
In theory I'd known all
Were sons of God above,
But I saw clearly then
We're brothers born of love.
I then began to live
By faith I'd long professed
And rose to brother all
Whom Jesus died to bless.

WHEN CHILDREN PRAY

When little children kneel to pray
I think God is not far away,
And softest prayers their lips intone,
I think reach up to heaven's throne.
And blest are parents day by day
Who teach their children how to pray,
For children's prayers are always heard
When offered up in children's words.
And every little child that prays
Redeems the earth in countless ways,
For children, kneeling, lisping prayers
Are of all gifts our nation shares,
The surest hope, the promise grand
That God will bless and spare this land.

TO POISON A CHILD

What if I with some poison
Defiled my children's food?
The courts would brand me *criminal*—
Unfit to be excused.
Yet I with impure thoughts
Can poison my child's mind,
And go on unsuspected
Of vilest deed unkind.
Yet poisoning children's food,
Or water that he's drinking,
Is certainly no more dangerous
Than poisoning children's thinking.

PUTTING BACK THE STARS

May friends remember me
As one who with his light
Lit every lamp he saw
While stumbling through this night;
As one who gladly did
A thousand thankless chores
'Til those shut out from love
Could pass through long-locked doors.
May friends remember me
And say of my replies,
"His words put back the stars
In our dark, faithless skies."

SPITE FENCE

With anger in my heart
I built one night a wall
Between my house and his,
And it was very tall.
I planned to see no more
The man I'd learned to hate,
And so I left no gap
To hang a friendly gate.
And though we met no more,
That fence, to my surprise,
Cast shadows on my lawn
And hid from me sunrise.

WHAT IS COURAGE?

I know what courage is:
It's fear that hums a tune;
It's doubt that offers prayers;
It's mirth in face of gloom.
It's tear-stained cheeks that smile
And calmness when you're cursed,
And courage is defeat
That quotes a scripture verse.
It's singing in the dark,
"The dawn will be so bright";
It's saying when you're blind,
"I see without my sight."
It's seamen tossed at sea
With nothing left to do
But shout above the storm,
"We'll hold the rudder true."

PETER'S SWORD

I wonder why he bought a sword
To slash the soldier's ear?
Could he have thought the Prince of Peace
Could win with sword or spear?
And did he think his deed would aid
The Kingdom to appear?
When will we learn Christ came to rid
The world of swords uncouth?
That He must purge the hearts of men
Blood red in claw and tooth?
Or else swords drawn defending Christ
Will kill the Prince of Truth?

MORE SAINTS NEEDED

I saw a saint today
Though saints are rather rare;
Yet he whom I beheld
Was not engaged in prayer.
Instead he was at work
In common working clothes,
And as he worked he sang
With face and eyes that glowed.
He sang a song of faith
And was to God's grand cause
A channel of His love,
A saint in overalls.

IF GOD SHOULD GRANT MY HEART'S DESIRE

I've craved no house beside the road,
I'm sure I never will;
I seek a quiet sequestered spot—
A house high on a hill.
I long to get away from things
And on some hilltop tarry,
Until I feel God's presence near,
And darkness floods the valley.
Then grant me such a house and let
Me go apart and stand
In presence of unhurried things,
Far from the cries of man,
And I'll arise each morn refreshed,
At peace with man and God,
And turn my steps back to the city
Where sad men, friendless, plod.
I'll stand where troubled souls rush by
And be a friend to them,
If God should grant my heart's desire—
A hilltop house with Him.

IS CHRISTMAS A JOKE?

During college years, my roommate and I planned a surprise birthday party for Herb, a mutual friend. After arrangements were made and invitations were issued we waited expectantly for the day to arrive.

About thirty enthusiastic friends came that night to help celebrate Herb's birthday. Suddenly we realized we had failed to arrange for the appearance of the honored guest. Thinking he would be in his usual place, we went in search of him. He could not be found and none knew of his whereabouts.

Returning to the party scene we suggested it be called off inasmuch as the guest of honor was not available. Some suggested the party be held in his absence. When this was agreed upon, games, refreshments and all were entered upon with hilarity. A cake adorned with twenty-one candles was lit as all sang jovially, "Happy birthday, dear Herb." It all seemed like a big joke. The master-of-ceremonies, holding a gift our combined resources had purchased, made a presentation speech. Laughter welcomed every remark he made. When he had said all he could, realizing there was no one to accept the gift, he said, "I think we've taken this joke as far as we can."

Thirty giggling party-goers left the dining hall that night. When my roommate and I left, we left bewildered, with big lumps in our throats. On the next day when we told this story to Herb, our absent guest, he, too, thought it was a joke. Indeed, it was just that.

Is not Christmas Christ's birthday? Yet in many homes He has been left out, unwelcome and uninvited, during Christmas festivities. Lest we lose the meaning of His birthday and make Christmas a cheap joke, may we be very sure the honored Guest is invited and welcome.